Woman of Persistent Faith

Surviving through the darkest night to behold
the beauty of a brighter day

Akiesha "Keke" Taylor

Woman of Persistent Faith

Surviving through the darkest night to behold
the beauty of a brighter day

Akiesha "Keke" Taylor

T&J PUBLISHERS

A Small Independent Publisher With A Big Voice

Printed in the United States of America by
T&J Publishers (Atlanta, GA.)
www.TandJPublishers.com

© Copyright 2016 by Akiesha Taylor

All rights reserved. This book or parts thereof may not be reproduced in any form, stored in a retrieval system, or transmitted in any form by any means-electronic, mechanical, photocopy, recording, or otherwise-without prior written permission of the publisher, except as provided by United States of America copyright law.

All Bible verses used are from the King James Version (1982) by Thomas Nelson, Inc., The New International Version (NLT), and The English Standard Version (ESV).

SECOND EDITION
Author: Akiesha Taylor
Editor: Marcey Bush, A Way with Words Communications & Publishing, LLC

Cover design by Timothy Flemming, Jr. (T&J Publishers)
Book format and layout by Timothy Flemming, Jr. (T&J Publishers)

Photography by Yolanda Norman Rouse (www.yolandarouse.com)

ISBN: 978-0-9981621-1-9

To contact author, go to:
akieshat@gmail.com
Facebook: Akiesha K Taylor
Instagram: keketaylor7

ACKNOWLEDGMENTS

This book was written from a hard place in my life; a place where I've never thought I would escape from; a place where I was contemplating suicide; a place of pain and rejection; it was at the lowest place I could possibly be. In this place, God met me! I would like to thank GOD for His grace, mercy, forgiveness, and infinite love.

To my mother, Faye: Thank you for all that you have done in Quan's life. Thank you for trying your best as a single parent to raise three kids. To my brothers, Jamaal and Hakim, and to my sisters-in-love, my nieces and nephews, I love you.

To my God-Parents: The late Mrs. Jones - I thank GOD for allowing you to be in my life. You loved me, forgave me, taught me, and helped me to become the young lady that I am today. Mr. Jones, I'm so blessed to have you by my side throughout all of these years.

To my leaders: Thanks to my first pastor in Sandersville, GA., Elder Mark & Faye Walden, who introduced me to COGIC. Thank you for your biblical teachings throughout the years. Bishop Mark & Dorothy Walden, thank you for loving Quan and myself. Thank you for all of your prayers and encouragement throughout the years! We are blessed to have anointed leaders like you.

To all my aunts, uncles and cousins in NJ, DE, VA, NC, GA and FL., I Love each of you.

To my late grandmothers: Lucille (NaNa) and Hattie (Grandma), I miss you two; but I'm blessed to have had two godly women to model after.

To Prophet Kennebrew: Thank you for your prayers and being led by GOD.

To Thomas: Thank you for all that you do.

To Terry Ann Phillips: Thank you for hosting your "Saved and Fabulous" brunch. It was God's divine timing that we met at your brunch. GOD allowed me to meet Jackie! Your ministry is going to take you places you've never imagined.

To Jackie Flemming: You are such an inspiration to me and to so many young ladies. Thank you for allowing me to work with your husband to get my story told and published. I look forward with working with the two of you in the future.

To Timothy Flemming, Jr. and T&J Publishers: You are GOD sent. I know I sent numerous emails back to back, worrying about the deadline; anxious and excited. I'm proud of your work and talent.

Marcey Bush: You're simply amazing! Thank you for taking the time to immerse yourself in this book. The grace that you showed with the revision is remarkable. As you took the time to pour into this book, I pray in return that God will bless you one hundredfold.

To those who want to give up: Don't! You have a story to tell! Don't allow the enemy to distract you!

In memory of my father, the late Leroy Thompson, Jr.

To my hero: my son, Quan

I'm blessed that GOD entrusted and chose me to be your mother. I am Blessed to have you in my life. Thank you for encouraging me when you would see me cry at night. I admire your walk with GOD and your faith, and how you would remind me that we would make it through the rough spots in our lives. You are going to be an awesome Pediatric Neurosurgeon!

*God didn't promise days without pain,
laughter without sorrow,
or sun without rain,
but He did promise strength for the day,
comfort for the tears,
and light for the way.
If God brings you to it,
He will bring you through it.*

- Anonymous

Table of Contents

Introduction: Giving Birth To The Journey — 13

Chapter One: Black Sheep — 19

Chapter Two: Angels — 27

Chapter Three: The Sacrifice — 33

Chapter Four: The Report — 41

Chapter Five: The Breaking Of Dawn — 49

Chapter Six: Desperation — 59

Chapter Seven: The Dream — 65

Chapter Eight: Coming Out Of Darkness — 79

Chapter Nine: Conversations With God — 91

Introduction

GIVING BIRTH TO THE JOURNEY

IT WAS ON JUNE 17, 1997, THAT I WAS ADMITTED INTO A very distinguished club, one that's exclusive to women: motherhood. The nearly unbearable, indescribable pain that I endured during this process was my rite of passage into this exclusive club. My mother, a veteran member of the club, was there in the hospital room with me, along with my son's father. Her presence was both a source of warmth and coldness, typical of our sometimes-complicated dynamic. Both she and my son's father were anxiously awaiting the arrival of my firstborn child.

While I lay in that hospital bed, I could see fear and wonder in my mother's eyes. She didn't have to say a word;

her eyes did the talking. I could pick up that part of her that was excited about the fact that I was about to give birth to a baby, but the other part of her was nervous about what this meant for me. There was a sense of worry in her eyes over the life-altering consequences that this baby would have on my life. She was a woman who knew struggle, a woman who knew pain. Her heart was a deep ocean of unspoken secrets which she had to bear alone as a single parent, a hidden chamber filled with thoughts she had to conceal behind a fabricated smile many days. I would soon come to know this struggle. I would soon come to learn this craft.

For months I had been feeling little feet, elbows, and knees pressing against the inner wall of my bulging belly. It was still shocking and somewhat weird that a little person was inside of me, growing and moving about as if excited and anxiously waiting to break free and experience the world. I had spent so many days and nights of my life wondering about him: *Will he look like me or his father? Will he have dimples? What will his personality be like? Will he be quiet? Outgoing? Humorous? Serious?* So many similar questions ran through my mind during my pregnancy. But there were also many fears and concerns that ran through my mind, mainly about myself: *Am I ready to be a mother? Am I capable of loving this beautiful little boy like he deserves to be loved? What other sacrifices will I have to make in order to be a good mother to this child? What will others think of me as a single parent? Did I make the right decision to keep this child, or should I have taken the advice of others around me?*

I remember the moment that everything became real to me. Up until the precise moment that it was time to give

Introduction: Giving Birth To The Journey

birth, everything still seemed like somewhat of a dream to me. I remember asking myself, *Is this really happening? Am I really about to become a mom? Me?!* I saw the movies, read the books, and had become familiar with the many stories written by mothers pertaining to giving birth—by first-time mothers, by young mothers. But no amount of preparation could ease the anxiety of being in the position where I was actually about to give birth. *This is really happening*, I thought to myself as I watched the midwives and the doctor get into their positions. The moment was upon us to bring this baby into the world. It was real now, no longer dreamy, no longer surreal.

The intensity of the nervousness and anxiety I felt at that moment could only be matched by the amount of pain my body was in. The pain of those contractions hitting my body was like the steady pounding of the waves of a sea hammering a shoreline during a hurricane. It was an indication that I was close to giving birth, close to witnessing a miracle. Pain serves this purpose in so many capacities in life. The birth of a dream, the manifestation of a hope, the answer to a yprayer – they are all heralded by some type of pain. And perhaps, the greater the pain, the bigger the miracle, as some would say.

It was now too late to turn back. The baby was on its way. He was coming. Whether or not I was truly ready for it, I was now committed. I was in for the long nights filled with cries and the moments filled with exhaustion because of lack of sleep. Culprits like nursing, changing, burping, and everything else that goes along with taking care of a baby were now my lot. I was now committed to the many years of sacrifice, the many years of investing, the many years of struggle that lay ahead.

While I was experiencing the pain of the contractions, one of the midwives grabbed my hand and began whispering instructions in my ear: "Breathe. Relax. Breathe. Take a deep breath. NOW PUSH!!!!!"

There is something extraordinary that happens during the birthing process. You discover a strength you didn't know you had, you do things you didn't know you could do, and you bear things you didn't think you could bear. Your body stretches as much as it needs to. You discover that you were built for those moments that seem too incredible to face, built for those challenges that seem too difficult to overcome. There is nothing that anyone can give you or has the capacity to give you in order for you to succeed in accomplishing your purpose in life because… you were built for this.

"PUSH!!!!!" the midwife yelled.

"I can do this! I can do it!" I reminded myself. "I got this!" Once more, I pushed, then took a break, took a couple of quick breaths, and then jumped right back in and pushed some more. Veins were bulging out of my neck and forehead, sweat was pouring off me, and tears were streaming down the side of my face. Push! Breathe! Push! Then finally, the top of the baby's head had become visible.

I mustered up what little strength I had left in my body and gave it all I had. I pushed with all my might. Finally, suddenly, I heard the sweetest sound: the sound of my baby crying. There he was, my beautiful baby boy. Upon beholding this gift, every one of my fears, worries, and anxieties ceased. The nagging thoughts and questions became silent. I had no doubt in my mind that a new chapter in my life had started and that my life would never be the same from that point forward.

Introduction: Giving Birth To The Journey

I had no doubt in my mind that I made the right choice. June 17, 1997, would be a day etched in the annals of eternity as the day that my life changed forever. It was the day that I brought my son, Quan, into the world. He would change my life and the lives of those around him in so many ways. His journey would become my inspiration, and it would also remind the countless others around him that we can do the impossible when we put our faith in God.

Quan was more than just a child; he was a special needs child. This made the challenge all the more difficult. But love made me accept and embrace the challenge, and it gave me the strength to persevere to the end. It taught me how to bury secret pains in the ocean of my heart and conceal hidden thoughts in the secret chambers of my soul behind a plastered smile, too. Quan's challenges would become my challenges. I would cry not only my tears but his also. I would feel not only my pain but his also. But in the end, I would discover the power of enduring love and faith in God. In the end, I would discover that miracles literally happen in this world. Yes, miracles! I would discover that you can survive things you think you can't survive and you can endure things you think you can't endure. Trust me when I tell you, if you hold on to your faith in God, you will eventually witness gloom turn into glory and tragedy into triumph. God will give you the grace to endure until the end, until the miraculous takes place.

This is the story of a survivor. This is my story... and your roadmap to a miracle.

Chapter 1
BLACK SHEEP

I CAME INTO THIS WORLD ON JULY 11, 1978, IN NEWARK, New Jersey. I was a proud summer baby. Bouncing. Happy. Full of life. Not one to allow a dull moment to slip up in my mother's home. Like every child, I enjoyed the innocence afforded me at birth, but I eventually came to discover that it came with an expiration date. I would not be allowed to meander through life's terrain for long with my head in a cloud of oblivion. At some point, I would discover that life is hard, that it can be tough, that it can come with a world of pain in the palms of its hands.

My mother was a hardworking woman. She was like the typical hardworking mothers I had seen growing up: strong, firm, mean out of necessity, highly protective. She was a single mother carrying a heavy load on her delicate shoulders. She had to look after me, my siblings, and herself. And as single mothers do, she did what she had to do to make sure food was on the table each night.

My mother also had two sons, for a total of three children—and each of us had different fathers. She always seemed to be stressed out, but she would eventually find a way to deal with her stress – she would take it out on me. Verbal abuse became the norm to me throughout my childhood. Over time, I grew accustomed to hearing a barrage of insults from my mother who struggled to find ways to cope with the pain of abandonment and disappointment eating away at her delicate heart. She was a precious woman, a gentle woman at times, but the softness of her heart was hidden behind the calluses of self-preservation. I realized that my mother wanted to be a good mother. She wanted to love me. She always took care of my material needs, but to express love was something with which she wrestled. She just didn't know how. She only knew how to be abusive, both verbally and physically.

My father was somewhat active in my life. He wasn't entirely in nor out of the picture. He would stop by my mother's house to see me from time to time. He just wasn't a regular in my life the way every child hopes for. The times that I would see him, I could tell that there was something wrong with him. I didn't quite understand what it was about him that had my mother so concerned, nor why he and my mother just couldn't be in the same house under the same roof together. Why couldn't they just be a couple, and why couldn't we simply be a family?

As a child, I couldn't understand why my dad didn't want to be in my life, why he didn't want to be there to fill that void in my heart. It would be years later that I would

Chapter 1: Black Sheep

discover the reality of drug addiction. I would later come to understand the power that drugs can have over a person and just how much they can change a person's life. Despite my father's good intentions, he was enslaved to drugs; they were his master and they controlled every aspect of his life, ravaging his heart and mind like a cancer.

For years I watched my father stumble in and out of my life. I watched him move nearly zombie-like at the beck and call of the drugs, compelled and driven by an appetite he couldn't control. He had been stolen from me. He had been stolen from my mom. He did what he could to help—he brought me things I needed and wanted whenever he'd visit. But he left out the most important thing: himself.

SAYING "GOODBYE"

The day seemed normal enough, no different than any other day. The power of the sun seemed to chase away the dark clouds in my mind, clouds that hovered over my tattered soul. It was a soul suffering from the effects of a childhood rife with broken dreams, broken promises, and broken relationships. I was at home playing with my dolls when suddenly, the doorbell rang. My mother answered the door and there stood my uncle from North Carolina. He made the long drive all the way to New Jersey when he received the news that my father (his brother) was in the hospital. My father had been in hospitals before, but this had to be a serious situation for my uncle, along with his other siblings, to travel all the way to New Jersey. He told me that my father was asking to see me at the hospital, that it was urgent that he see me while he still had time. My uncle took me to University Hospital where my father was. When we made it to the room where my dad was, my uncle motioned for me to go in. I didn't know what to expect. When I entered, I saw my father and his mother, Hattie. Grandmother Hattie was a sweet, loving, God-fearing woman. She had a look on her face that indicated she knew this would perhaps be the last time she would see her son. I was shocked to see my father in the state he was in. He didn't look like the man I had seen on so many occasions. This was a totally different man. He looked horrible. His complexion was darker. He had lost most of his weight. He looked so sick and so small, his skin merely clinging to his bones. He was emaciated and had to muster up the strength to speak. Even then, his words were few.

He reached out his hand when he saw me, and nervously, I walked over to him and placed my hand in his. I could feel the chill, the coldness of death in his hands. He then looked me in the eyes and said, "I love you. Be a good girl." I could see in his eyes that he wanted to say more, so much more. His eyes were full of the words he wanted to speak throughout the years but couldn't because of the drugs that had him bound; they were full of the words he wanted to speak to me at that moment but couldn't because death had him bound. In this weakened state, it was as if he was thinking about all the time he wanted to share with me, all the times he wanted to be a father but couldn't. His silence was louder than his words.

After our brief time together, I left my father's room and went to sit down beside all my other uncles and aunts in the hospital waiting room. They were loving, but secretive, not willing to reveal to me everything that was going on. At the time, I didn't know why my father was dying. But as it was

Chapter 1: Black Sheep

later revealed to me, he was in the relentless grip of AIDS. He had contracted the disease as a result of using an infected needle. That day at the hospital was the last I saw of him. That would be the last time we spoke, for on the next day, he passed away. He died on his birthday – July 28, 1989. He was only 38 years old.

"GOODBYE" AGAIN

In 1993, my mother decided to relocate back to Sandersville, Georgia, but while in New Jersey, we all lived with my grandmother (whom I called Nana). She was a kind and understanding woman. Her arms were like a shield of sun, blocking out the darkness that surrounded me as a little girl, just waiting to devour me. Her whispers in my ear were so soothing to my soul, so reassuring that I was loved, that I would be alright despite what was happening in my life. She was such a source of strength in my life. Her words to me were always encouraging, always uplifting. I loved being in her presence. When my mom decided to move out of her mother's house, I asked her if I could stay behind and live with my Nana instead. I was elated that she said yes. While my mother and my two brothers relocated back to Georgia, I stayed behind in New Jersey with Nana where I was happy.

Several months had passed since my mom moved back to Georgia, and while living with Nana, I was at peace. I seemed not to have a care in this world. But tragedy wasn't done hounding me. One morning I received one of those phone calls people dread receiving. I got a call from the hospital telling me that Nana had to be admitted because she had suffered cardiac arrest. And it was shortly thereafter that she passed away. She died in May of 1994.

Many thoughts ran through my mind during this time. I thought often about Nana, her smile, her gentle voice and kind words. I thought about the sunshine she seemingly emitted from her pores into my soul, how she lit up my life. I thought about the fact that it was now all over and that I would have to go back to living with my mom. The contrast, I suspected, would be as stark as night and day. At Nana's house, it was day; but now, it was time to make my home among the darkness. *Maybe*, I thought to myself, *going to Georgia to live with my mom might not be so bad.* This might be an opportunity for us to build a good relationship, to start off fresh and establish that mother-daughter relationship I always desired. I decided to look at the bright side and take on a positive attitude.

In August of 1994, I moved from New Jersey to Sandersville, Georgia, to live with my mom. When I arrived, things looked a lot different. Sandersville, Georgia was no New Jersey. The area was a lot different from what I was used to. Even the people seemed different. This wasn't a big city environment. It wasn't busy or fast-paced; instead, Sandersville was a slow, small, country town. This was a new culture. I would have to make all new friends. *This will take a bit of getting used to*, I thought to myself. The biggest adjustment, however, wouldn't be the one I had to make in the outside world; it would be the one I had to make inside my mother's home.

LOOKING FOR A LIGHT

During the first few days and weeks living with my mom, ev-

Chapter 1: Black Sheep

erything went really well. Mom and I got along good. She was kind, nice, and respectful towards me, but things gradually began to change. My mom slowly began to go back to her old ways of cursing me, insulting me, and calling me out of my name. After a while, it was back to the "You ugly black b*tch!!" "Listen here, you black @#&%!!" insults. I was called "black this, black that" so much that I began to see myself as the black sheep of the family.

Shame began to creep into my soul. At times, I would internalize all the insults my mom was dishing out and see myself as ugly, unworthy, unfit, undeserving, and unwanted. It was difficult for me to hold my head up or feel good about myself. Depression began to grip my soul. My grades in school began to decline. Yes, I was back in the grip of darkness, and now Nana wasn't around to chase away its brooding aura. At times, desperation would take hold of me and compel me to leave the house in search of relief. I just needed someone to talk to… anyone! I was screaming within. I was sinking into a pit of mental darkness and crying out for help. Thoughts and suggestions began to cross my mind: run away; drink alcohol; take drugs. I had seen the effects of drugs and other dangerous substances on ethe lives of those around me. Drugs had robbed me of a father; they had ravaged his life and controlled him like a harsh, heartless, and cruel taskmaster. I knew early on in life that this path led to even more misery than what I was already in. So I chose to follow a different path: I began to cry out to God. And I discovered something… that He both hears and answers.

Woman Of Persistent Faith

Chapter 2
ANGELS

It felt good visiting The House of God Church of God in Christ (COGIC) every 1st and 3rd Sunday. The choir would thunder in that church every Sunday morning, and I would simply bask in the glory of the moment, enraptured in the nearly palpable excitement charging the air. Being in church definitely beat being in the streets, in jail, or in the grave. This was a place away from home where I could find peace of mind and refuge from the many problems waiting patiently for me at home. Church became one of my main outlets. Staying involved in things around the church helped me to take my mind off my problems and stay busy, which was a positive thing.

If there is one thing I learned in church, it was the importance of prayer. I also gained the realization that God is personally involved in the lives of those who trust Him. This was a revolutionary concept to me as a child. I couldn't see God, nor could I touch Him or smell Him, but I could believe that He was literally right by my side everywhere I went, that He was witnessing everything I was going through, and that His heart ached whenever I shed tears of pain and sadness. It was amazing to hear the preacher say that God is that close, that intimate, and that personal with each and every one of His children. As it was explained to me: God isn't "the man upstairs," but rather, He is "a friend that sticks closer than a brother." The one thing that was said that really struck home with me was when the preacher said we're supposed to refer to God as "Father," according to the Bible. That, perhaps, left the biggest impression on me and made me feel a closeness to God like never before. A father was what I craved. The hole in my heart was left by a father, and it could only be filled by a father.

At night, I would pray for God to heal my heart from the hurt and pain. I would picture Him next to me in my room as I slept. This thought gave me great comfort each day and each night. I later began to see evidence of God's hand in my life in subtle ways as time progressed.

THE LOVELY MRS. JONES

Although my mother and I never really developed the type of closeness that I longed for throughout my years as a child, I was blessed to have another mother figure in my life who filled that void. After the passing of my grandmother, I felt so alone. But it was around that time that I came to know a woman named Mildred Jones. Mrs. Jones and her husband all but legally adopted me into their family. Unofficially, I was

Chapter 3: The Sacrifice

their daughter—they treated me as such. Mrs. Jones and her husband didn't have any children of their own due to complications she experienced with regards to childbearing, so they adopted a son and also took me in as the daughter they never had.

I remember reading a Bible verse that says, "Don't forget to show hospitality to strangers, for some who have done this have entertained angels without realizing it!" (Hebrews 13:2 NLT) When I think about how I met Mrs. Jones, I recall how I would, as a little girl in elementary school, volunteer to help in so many ways around the school. I volunteered as an assistant to the principal, would offer any assistance to teachers, and would go down to the cafeteria and talk to the cafeteria workers all the time. This put me in Mrs. Jones' line of sight. I loved to interact with people, and without even realizing it, through my interactions, I would end up becoming "Sunshine" to a woman who needed a daughter and she'd end up becoming "mom" to a little girl who needed a mother. We needed each other.

I met Mrs. Jones while in the 6th grade in New Jersey. She was a very perceptive woman. Upon getting acquainted with me, she was able to easily pick up on the fact that things were shaky with me at home. She detected that my heart was full of hurt and pain and my self-image was pretty tarnished. Therefore, she became that angel who seized every opportunity to inject words of encouragement into my famished soul, and I appreciated every moment of it. I became her "Sunshine"—that was her nickname for me.

Mrs. Jones worked in the cafeteria as the lunchroom lady. When she first saw me, she instantly took to me. Whenever I'd go to lunch, I made sure to speak to her. I would also stop by to see her whenever I had free time. She would always take the time to talk to me, to listen to me, to check up on me like a parent. She believed in me and knew I was fully capable of doing excellent in school, but she also knew how to step in as a motherly figure without making my mother feel threatened. Due to the sensitive nature of my relationship with my mom, Mrs. Jones realized that her actions could have either exacerbated a bad situation or diffused it. She chose the latter. "How are those grades, young lady?" Mrs. Jones would ask. "You can do better than this," she'd utter whenever I didn't do as good as I could have on a test or quiz. Sensing that the stress of my home life was a factor in my poor performance in school, Mrs. Jones opted to keep me focused instead on my autonomy as an individual. By doing so, she helped me realize that regardless what transpired at home, my future was entirely mine. I needed that push. I needed that reminder... and often. I needed that perspective. But most of all, I needed someone to believe in me. Mrs. Jones did that. Regardless of how many times I was told at home that I was a nobody and that I'd never amount to anything in life, Mrs. Jones knew how to counter those destructive words with a gentle display of love and acceptance. She never once said a bad word against my mother; she simply let me know I had a second mother that was there for me whenever I needed her.

God works in mysterious ways. I know now the meaning of the words we often sing in church: "God is a mother to the motherless and a father to the fatherless."

Originally from North Carolina, Mrs. Jones and her husband moved back there from New Jersey in 1998m.

Chapter 3: The Sacrifice

Though the two of us stayed in contact with each other even while she was living in New Jersey, it was a blessing when she was closer to me. We never lost touch. Throughout my years in middle school and high school, I would still get those questions: "How are your grades?" "Are you focusing like you're supposed to?" I also continued to receive those admonishments such as "Now, don't let those little knucklehead boys mess you up! They only want one thing from you!"

Mrs. Jones and her husband used her savings to purchase my first car for me – a 1995 Ford Taurus. They drove it all the way down from North Carolina to Georgia to surprise me with it. That was one of the best days of my life. That car was truly needed because of the hectic schedule I was under at that time in my life. God knew that I needed it... among other things. That wasn't the extent of Mr. & Mrs. Jones' impact in my life. Those two were constants in my life, people who showed me over and over what real love was.

OTHER ANGELS

There were also other people who God sent to help me during my times of need. As I stated earlier, my family didn't have a lot of money. We struggled just to get the bare necessities. So, as you can imagine, non-essentials (seen as luxuries in my house) were simply out of the question. In my case, many of the extra programs and activities around school were luxuries, including the prom. My mother would do what she could, but that usually wasn't enough whenever finances were involved. I was, therefore, blessed to have others who didn't mind stepping in and helping to shoulder the cost of things I needed and things that were important to me. For example, one of my teachers purchased my prom dress for me, another paid for my corsage, and my cousin blessed me with the shoes to go with my prom dress. I felt like Cinderella. Though I was poor and underprivileged, I was blessed by those whom God placed around me. They helped me to experience happiness like no other. I felt favored. It was as if anytime I had an important need, someone would suddenly appear to meet it. I didn't have to want for anything. I knew that this was not by coincidence, but rather, it was the hand of Divine Providence in action.

Chapter 3
THE SACRIFICE

GRADUATION TIME HAD COME. I MADE IT! IT WAS TIME to say goodbye to high school. I'd enjoyed it while it lasted. I was going to miss the pep rallies, the football and basketball games, and all the other activities at school. My friends and I talked about our plans for the future more often than not. In my plans, I saw myself going off to college, graduating, moving up the ladder in the corporate world, making good money, coming back and taking care of my mother, and then settling down and getting married to a good man, having a few kids, and living happily ever after. And it seemed as if I was on my way there. Things were already looking up for me after high school.

    I graduated with good grades because I hunkered down and focused. Thank God for those teachers who took a special interest in me and made sure I didn't fall behind. More importantly, thank God for Mrs. Jones who wouldn't ease off me until I finished school. So many people had invested in me, including many at the church I was attending. My pastor at the time, Elder Mark Walden, was excited about my future. Many of the members there at the church were excited about my future. It was as if I now had my own cheerleading squad behind me, rooting me on. They witnessed my pain and my humble beginnings, my struggles and my perseverance, and now they were rejoicing with me as they saw the light at the end of the tunnel of my plight.

At first, the weight of such high expectations didn't seem to really bother me; it was exciting to me. It was as if I had been doused in lights like a superstar. But responsibility is a big part of the picture. Being under the weight of high hopes means bearing a great responsibility. At times, you become a symbol for those who feel their seasons have passed and gone and are now looking to vicariously live out their dreams and hopes through you. I was under a lot of pressure.

I remember when that Sunday morning came around and it was time to engage in the long-held ritual of honoring the graduates during our church service. I was truly excited about having my name called; I was nearly as excited that Sunday morning as I was during my actual graduation ceremony. The excitement was bubbling up on the inside of me, not just because of where and what I was leaving but because of where I was going. When my name was called, it was acknowledged that not only did I successfully graduate from high school with high marks but that I had also been accepted into Liberty University in West Virginia. For everyone in the church, that was the most exciting news. That's what I

CHAPTER 4: THE REPORT

was most excited about. All the hard work and the investment placed in me by those who loved me had paid off. I was about to go off to college, and my education was fully paid for. All I would have to do was keep my grades up and maintain a certain grade point average (GPA), which would be easy enough for me to do; after all, I was driven. I had developed a work ethic that would make matriculating through college easy. Most of all, I was determined that nothing was going to stop me from succeeding. I refused to let anyone or anything get in my way. I was on my way to the stars above, ready to tackle life with the force of a 300-pound linebacker. The sky was the limit. I was on my way! Until...

DETOUR ON THE WAY TO THE STARS

In 1996, a hit song by Tupac, KC and JoJo entitled "How Do You Want It?" filled the airways. That was also the year when all of us young girls were running around singing "You're the One" by SWV (Sisters with Voices).

I was now 18 years old and feeling the vibe while hanging out with this young man who found his way into my life. It was around graduation timer, and I had seen him around the apartment complex where I lived, but I never really said anything to him. His cousin lived in the same complex with me, and he would come over a lot, but whenever he came over, he would never really say anything to me.

All of that changed one day when he came over. I came home from school and that handsome dude (whom I'll refer to as "Mike") was just hanging around outside. When he saw me this time, he spoke. I tried not to give away that I was attracted to him., but I did ask him if he would drive me to the CVS store—I didn't have a car back then and I needed to pick up a few items for myself. He drove me to the store and we chatted and got to know each other a little. Over the next few days, weeks, and months, we got to know each other even more. Eventually, we started dating. I quickly fell in love with him. We began a relationship that lasted over several years, one filled with some serious ups and downs, one that took my life in a different direction than I had planned.

Perhaps it was the music. Perhaps it was just the moment we were wrapped up in. I was feeling him, and he was feeling me. We were gazing into each other's eyes as if nothing else mattered, as if time and space had been suspended. We acted as if there was only the beating of our hearts and the longing for each other's embrace. As our hungry eyes ogled each other, we figured, *We'll make this a night to remember.* And that's just what we did! That cool night in November would become an unforgettable one.

It was that November night when Mike and I had unprotected sex and conceived our first child, Quan. We were just two young people enraptured in a moment… one that would cost us a lifetime. I didn't expect to get pregnant. I certainly didn't plan to get pregnant. I thought we were careful and safe. But truth be told, all sexual intimacy carries a price—for women, that price is often pregnancy. As I learned (all too late), girls have to be a bit more cautious with their bodies lest they end up dealing with morning sickness alone, visiting OB/GYN clinics alone, facing the midnight food cravings alone, and dealing with the many other things that come along with pregnancy alone… including the shame you feel when everyone who believed in you suddenly feels a sense

CHAPTER 4: THE REPORT

of disappointment when they look at you now.

I had to live with the idea that the church girl whose future was once bright was now at a crossroads because of one night of passion in November. Thank God Mike was not a coward when it came to handling his responsibility; he did step up to the plate. He was there to check on me and to provide the support I needed during my pregnancy. He was, undoubtedly, nervous about the baby and even about his own future. Sure, he had dreams and goals also. I'm quite certain he didn't envision himself living in a low-income apartment complex in the country all his life. He, too, wanted to make it out of our humble beginnings and experience the world, living life to the fullest while seeing his dreams come to pass. But we knew that we both had a tough decision to face now. Would we put our lives on hold and focus on the baby or choose...

THE ALTERNATIVE

There I was, weighing my options: a baby or a career; a baby or a life filled with the freedom to explore, to come and go as I wish; a baby or college. Equally as troubling was the fact that I really didn't know if Mike and I had an actual future together. We came together for the baby, but whether we'd make it as a couple remained to be seen. I didn't want our son to grow up in a broken home, which was a big fear of mine. That was a pain that I endured and didn't intend to pass on to my son. I wanted him to at least see both a father and a mother together under the same roof loving each other faithfully. That was my dream as a little girl. That was a reality drugs robbed me of. That was the least that I could give my child.

In the upcoming months, Mike began to be less romantic. Perhaps, it was just the nature of things. When people start to get comfortable around each other, sometimes theyl begin to look less impressive. The things that initially draw two people together can easily become forgotten with time. Keeping fires burning is a task that must be and can be learned but only by two individuals who are willing to put in the work and grow together. I wanted to grow with Mike and spend the rest of my life with him. I saw him as the love of my life, the only one for me. I had big dreams that included the two of us, but I wasn't sure what he had in mind. And as time progressed, I would become less confident in our future together. My mother sensed the despair that I was in. She realized what this baby meant for my budding future. She knew all the pain, shame, heartache, and headache that would come along with a baby, so she offered me the one solution that she and I were certain would remedy the situation: an abortion. She wasn't the only person to mention this as an option. There were several people who whispered into my ears this piece of advice. They reminded me that if I kept the baby, I would have to miss out on my opportunity to go to college, and college was such a big part of my master plan to take my life to the next level. College looked like my all and all, like the definitive key to unlocking countless opportunities. I didn't want to fall into the category of those who were simply seen as a statistic, as a dependent waiting to be cared for by the state, as someone with no ambitions and expectations in life besides surviving. And growing up in the African-American community, it was almost considered a sin to not go to college or to be a college dropout. But I had a greater dilemma: go to college or go to hell.

Chapter 4: The Report

As a Christian, there was the deep conviction that abortion was a sin—it was murder, to be exact. I couldn't picture myself doing it. I couldn't see ending a life on account of keeping a scholarship as a viable option for me. I looked at life as being too precious, and I still do. To me, life is too valuable. A baby is too rare a blessing to toss away. I figured that college would always be around, but a life was, and is, simply too rare and too unique a thing to discard. Also, I really wanted to see what this little baby looked like and know who he'd take after. I had a lot of questions in my mind and found the journey that this child was going to put me on to be an intriguing one.

So, rather than disappoint God and myself, I chose to let others sit and simmer in their disappointment with me. I thought to myself, *Let them talk! This is my life! This is my body! Yes, this is my future! I will trust God even through my mistakes! Maybe the circumstances surrounding my pregnancy aren't perfect, but this child is a new chapter in not only my life, but in this world, and he deserves a right to live. Who's to say what this child may become? Who's to say what impact he might have on this world?* I realized that every life comes jam-packed with the potential to change the world, and that potential is only realized in light of the selfless act of a parent who possesses this revelation and perspective. I gave up college that year. I turned down a full scholarship to Liberty University. I turned down the opportunity to travel and spend the next four years enjoying the college life. I chose to make a sacrifice (not for my sake, but for the sake of my unborn son, Quan), believing in the extraordinary power of love and the ability of God to change the world and change lives using a single life... even if that world and life was simply mine.

Chapter 4
THE REPORT

ORIGINALLY, QUAN WAS SCHEDULED TO BE BORN ON July 28, 1997 (my father's birthday), but he came earlier than planned. He was born at 36 weeks rather than the full 40 weeks, a whole month early. He weighed in at 5 pounds 2 ounces. Amazingly, he didn't have to be held in ICU because he was completely healthy.

When I first saw Quan, my heart was overwhelmed by the joy I felt. It was nearly indescribable. To see those little eyes, little feet, that head full of hair, that beautiful brown skin... it was all so amazing. One look in his eyes and all my fears seemed to melt away. All the concerns I had about my future, about the opportunities I was sacrificing for Quan, they all vanished in an instant. I knew I made the right choice. I knew that choosing life for my son was the best decision I could have made. I just knew it. Something suddenly clicked inside of me while I lay in that hospital bed. It was a new revelation of my purpose and significance in life. A new chapter in my life had just begun. Suddenly, I developed a strength I had never possessed before and a resolve to do and be something I'd never done and become before.

I didn't care about the things I cared about before. My concern was now to be a mother, a provider, a protector, and a nurturer. Part of my purpose in life was now to raise up a son, a young man, to become a leader and a world shaker. Believe it or not, this gave me new impetus in the fight for significance and meaning in my own life. I now realized that I had to overcome certain of my own obstacles in life, not just for my sake but for the sake of the one who'd be following behind me – my son. With this revelation, I gained a strength to cast off the opinions and criticism of others. I cared less about what my mother thought or my son's father thought. I only cared about the needs of my son. I felt liberated.

YOUNG MOTHER

Mike brought the pampers and the milk and plenty of hugs and kisses for the baby. I stayed up late nights and early mornings nursing, changing diapers, getting peed on, burping the baby, and doing everything else that goes along with being a new mom. Everything seemed surreal. Truthfully, it was still sinking in that I was actually a mother, that I had a son now.

My mom was there for me like never before, helping to shoulder much of the responsibility. You could see the joy in her eyes also as she beheld her grandson. She just fell in love with him. To witness that kind of gentleness, that kind of delicateness and tenderness was refreshing to me—this being

Chapter 5: The Breaking Of Dawn

in stark contrast to the rough, brittle, tough demeanor I was used to witnessing out of her. Suddenly, a grandson shows up and her heart just melts like hot butter... at least for a few moments.

For several months, things seemed just fine. Quan was growing and gaining weight. Mike was involved. My mother was heavily involved with the baby. I was enjoying settling into my role as a new mom. I was getting the hang of things. And then, things took a sudden turn for the worse.

It was exactly five months after Quan was born that the accident happened. He somehow fell out of my bed and onto the floor despite the fact that the pillows surrounding him were positioned in such a way as to prevent him from falling out of the bed. Nevertheless, I was awakened in horror by the screams and cries of Quan as he lay on the floor. Immediately, I jumped up out of bed, picked Quan up, held him close to me, and then laid him down gently and got dressed. I then rushed him to the emergency room at our local hospital to get checked out. They performed a CT scan, did bloodwork on him, and ran tests. Afterward, they allowed us to return home, stating that there was no immediate danger, that Quan was healthy and okay. My heart was so relieved. My jangly nerves had finally calmed down. *Everything is going to be okay*, I told myself. We then settled in for the night.

The next morning, I got up out of bed and got ready to go to work. Everything seemed normal, nothing out of the ordinary. The tension from last night's scare had finally dissipated and it was back to the monotonous routine of day to day living. While at work, I received a phone call from Quan's pediatrician. I could hear the urgency in his voice as he informed me that it was imperative that I take Quan to the hospital—either the Medical College of Georgia in Augusta, Georgia, or the hospital in Macon, Georgia.

I decided to take Quan to the medical center in Augusta, Georgia. There, I was hit with some startling news. The neurosurgeon there at the medical center explained to me that the ventricle in Quan's brain was enlarged due to pressure and fluid on his brain. They instructed me to bring Quan back to the center the following Tuesday in order for them to give him a CT scan so that they could determine whether or not he was suffering from a hidden tumor in the brain or whether there was one that was developing in his brain. As the neurosurgeon was speaking, it felt as if my heart was sinking into a black hole. Fear gripped my soul. My mind was swirling with thoughts, fears, and worry... and this was only the beginning. I didn't know what to expect. I didn't know what to do besides follow the instructions of the doctors, trusting that they knew what was best in the situation. Even still, they were only human; neither of them was God— that's who I needed to hear from, who I needed to speak to. And somewhat to my surprise, He had much to say to me.

STRENGTH FOR THE JOURNEY

During my years growing up, there was one thing I learned, one principle that was drilled into my mind during all those days, weeks, and years of attending church services as a little girl: When you don't know where to turn, turn to God. As had been repeatedly stated, this tried and true method works best. In the normal course of the day, it seems natural to forget that there is a God who loves us, who watches over us, who

CHAPTER 5: THE BREAKING OF DAWN

waits for us to call upon Him; but crises have a way of reminding us of this reality. Not that I didn't believe in the power of prrayer – after all, I had experienced it firsthand. It's an incredible feeling you feel when you take a risk on something so abstruse as prayer only to see the literal results of it in the days gone by. I had experienced this feeling, this sensation, but now I was about to experience an even greater depth of the supernatural love of God. I was about to discover the meaning of "God knows, and He cares."

During the same week, I received the troubling report concerning Quan's health, my church, House of God Church of God in Christ, was in the midst of a week-long revival in Sandersville, Georgia. The guest revivalist was Prophet Kennebrew. Prophet Kennebrew was not just an ordinary preacher; he was an anointed prophet of God who operated in the supernatural power of the Holy Spirit. During service, Prophet Kennebrew began singling out different people in the audience to give prophetic (rhema) words to, and I happened to be one of those people. It was during that Friday night of the revival that Prophet Kennebrew called up both me and my son and began sharing with us a prophetic word from the Lord. He said that when I took Quan back to the hospital for his CT scan, the doctors would not find any tumors in his body. Such relief surged through my body when he said that to me! At that moment, I realized that things were going to be okay, that Quan didn't have a brain tumor, and most importantly, that God saw my hurt and pain and He was in the midst of my situation. That was undoubtedly the most important revelation I could have received because it strengthened me unlike anything else, letting me know that Quan's life was truly in God's hands and that his journey would not end at this point. Nothing could stop the tears of joy from streaming down my cheeks. I was wrapped in the presence of peace and tranquility. That night I slept knowing that Quan and I would go through storms in the coming days, but that we would come out on top in each and every trial we faced. One word from God was more than many opinions from doctors. I was now prepared to face whatever came my way.

Tuesday morning came. This was the day. While I was preparing to take Quan to the hospital, the words from Prophet Kennebrew kept playing in my head. Every time worry would try to arise in my soul, I would remind myself of what the prophet said. I had to combat a million negative thoughts using one revelation, that prophetic revelation being my only weapon in this internal struggle. I dressed Quan and the two of us were off to the hospital. Once there, the nurses and doctor began the process of running tests on Quan, searching for tumors. I watched patiently, vibrant hope eclipsing the fear in me. I knew everything was going to be alright. Test after test was administered. I waited and waited and waited. Finally, the doctor came into the room with the results from the scan: No tumor found! Those words sounded heavenly, nearly divine, to me.

After giving me the good news, the doctor then explained that there was still a problem. There was still a buildup of pressure and fluid on Quan's brain that needed to be dealt with. The doctor explained that as this pressure and fluid accumulated on his brain, Quan would become more and more irritable; he would cry more, be agitated more easily, and be uncomfortable, even experiencing great pain at times. They

Chapter 5: The Breaking Of Dawn

then admitted Quan into the hospital and diagnosed him with hydrocephalus, which is a buildup of too much cerebrospinal fluid in the brain—1 out of 1,500 children a year are born with this condition in the United States.

Sure, there was the constant temptation to ask, "Why my son?! Why Quan?!" Seemingly, just as one worry was put to rest, another one sprang up. It felt like a season of endless battles, of ups and downs, highs and lows. Troubling reports began to crash my soul like waves against a ship. In the upcoming days, I would begin to wonder, *When will the bad reports end? When will this struggle finally be over?* I would end up on my knees night after night. I'd have plenty more sleepless nights where I'd simply lay awake in my bed, staring up at the ceiling with my tears soaking my pillow. I'd lay there pondering the odds that my son happened to be the 1 out of 1,500 with this particular condition. In my mind, there was the question, *Why Quan?* But there was also the consideration that maybe Quan was chosen for this. All kinds of thoughts passed through my mind, but despite what I was thinking and feeling, there was only one assurance: God was with us. This put to rest the fears, worries, doubts, and questions running through my mind. That's all I had to go off. No matter how much my mind strayed from the internal assurance I had been given, it would always find its way back to that Friday night in that little church where I received the revelation that I needed in that season of my life. It was the report of the Lord that declared everything was going to be alright. That is the report I chose to believe; I *had* to believe.

Chapter 5
THE BREAKING OF DAWN

IN AN EFFORT TO DRAIN THE EXCESS FLUID FROM HIS BRAIN, Quan had to have a cerebral shunt placed to help move the fluid from his brain to other parts of his body n. A cerebral shunt is simply a valve that connects to a catheter which doctors insert into a person's body, usually just outside of their skull, right beneath the skin, around their ear. At first this worked fine in Quan, helping to drain some of that fluid around his brain. However, shunts sometimes malfunction, thereby requiring surgery for replacement, called a shunt revision.

While just a little baby, Quan had to undergo several surgeries to receive shunt revisions due to malfunctions. In order to replace the shunt in Quan's little body, the surgeon had to cut his head open and insert a valve in through his head and push it all the way down into his abdomen. It was painful just thinking about it, and it was even more painful knowing that Quan would have to endure this time and time again.

Quan had already received two shunt revisions, and it was time for him to receive his third. At that same time, my mother had to be hospitalized because of diabetes—she was in a coma. I found myself in the throes of a juggling act, one that took place in my heart and mind, as well as physically. It seemed I was constantly running back and forth between Quan and my mom.

I kept praying for my mother to recover and come out of her diabetic coma even while my son was undergoing surgery, believing as the Sunday School teachers and preachers would teach, that God is the only one who is omnipresent. "God, be with my mother. Heal my mother. Touch my mother's body, Lord," I prayed, all while I watched the surgeon make another incision in my son's head. I knew that either 1) I could allow doubt and fear and worry to tear me apart and perhaps put me in the hospital due to stress, or 2) I could learn to lean back, relax, and let go based on my confidence and belief in God and His power to do what I clearly could not do. I chose the latter. I stayed by my son's side during his surgery and afterward, and I also went to be by my mom's side during her sickness. I did only what I could do while trusting God to do the rest. I had to learn that I wasn't Superwoman. I had to accept that I am only human. That spared me great pain and suffering, especially in the days ahead.

SLEEPLESS IN SANDERSVILLE

The nights were long... and tough. Sleep deprivation became commonplace in my life during that season. There were times

Chapter 6: Desperation

when I barely rested at all during the night, having to look after Quan to ensure that the shunt was not malfunctioning while at the same time managing the regular responsibilities of motherhood and work. There was the pressure to be caretaker of a sick child while trying to salvage some semblance of a social life. Both my son and my mother were in recovery mode, and so much weight had fallen onto my shoulders that at times, I didn't know if I was coming or going, going or coming. Sometimes I felt as if I was in the Twilight Zone, my mind swirling round and round. People would have to snap me out of my daze, pull me out of a stupor.

No sleep.
A lot of work.
Little money.
Baby crying.
Rush to the hospital.
Mom needs medicine.
Running out of pampers.
Baby milk can empty; need more.
Gas light on in the car; need gas, but very little money left.
Boss riding my back at the job.
It's after 4 AM and I still haven't slept.
Got to get up before 7 AM—got to get ready to go to work.

The cycle was ongoing, continuous, day after day, week after week.

Mike and I were starting to have some problems. We were still together, but the relationship was starting to feel like a weight rather than an escape. We'd go out, and we'd both see about the baby, although I was the one who did so more. Those little rendezvous to the movies helped. Those evenings eating out helped a lot. Those little getaways took my mind off everything I was facing. They were like breaths of fresh air amidst the tumultuous waters of stress I kept sinking in.

My angel, Mrs. Jones was still around and very much active in my life during that time. I waited for her phone calls. She was always encouraging me to hold on and to not give up. She prayed with me on the phone and kept me reminded of God's presence, love, and power. I needed it because during that time, much of what I had learned as a little girl in church began to fall into the background of my life. It's not that my faith in God waned; it's just that my focus began to shift to other things, and being totally devoted and sold-out for Christ was no longer a priority.

THE FOURTH SURGERY

A year after Quan had his third shunt revision and my mother was diagnosed with diabetes, I experienced another big scare. One day Quan would not stop crying. He was terribly irritated all day and night. The next morning, I called the medical center and told them what was going on. At that point, the doctor instructed us to bring Quan in so that they could examine him and find out what was wrong. Quan's father and I immediately set out to drive him to the medical center 75 miles away, an hour and a half long drive. Amazingly, on that day, there was no real traffic on the road. Although speeding, we were not stopped by any police and all the lights happened to be green—it was a straight shot there. When we arrived at the medical center, we bypassed the emergency room and went

Chapter 6: Desperation

straight to the fourth floor to the neurosurgeon's office. The moment the neurosurgeon looked at Quan, he knew that there was something wrong. They immediately took a syringe and began draining fluid out from around Quan's brain right there in the hallway in the presence of other people. This seemed to be helping him, but then the doctors and nurses put Quan in a comatose state and placed him in ICU for three days.

While Quan was in ICU, I began to be suspicious of this particular medical center. I was tired of seeing my baby in the operating room getting cut on, and I began to wonder if these doctors were simply experimenting on my son to see what shunt procedure and treatment would work best. Was my son being used as a guinea pig? Repeatedly, the shunts they put in would malfunction. Did they really know what they were doing? At that point, I requested another neurosurgeon to perform Quan's surgery; however, that didn't remedy the problem because even that shunt malfunctioned at a later point, thereby requiring Quan to undergo yet another surgery. It was tiring… no, exhausting. But I was determined to see my son get better. I knew in my heart that we were going to make it through this season. That hope was all I had to go on.

WELCOME TO A CRUEL WORLD

It was time for Quan to enroll in school, and to be honest, it was the time period that I dreaded the most. I understood some of the issues that my son would be forced to endure. Because of the buildup of fluid on Quan's brain, he began to develop other problems that required therapy. Quan had to undergo physical, occupational, and speech therapy, as well as receive an Individualized Education Plan (IEP) and attend Special Ed classes. I knew that it was going to be a tough process for Quan to catch up in school because of his developmental delays, so I decided that I needed to take the lead in working with him before he even began taking his classes. I worked with him on his speech and would ask the therapist what type of exercises I could do with Quan at home to help him develop. I would order books that helped me as a parent to work with a special needs child. I did everything I could to get him ready for school and for life in general. The one thing I wanted to do more than anything else was establish a strong sense of identity in Quan, to let him know that he was loved, that he was valuable and significant, and that he could accomplish whatever goals he set out to accomplish. I wanted him to know that God loved him and had a very special plan for his life. These things I knew Quan wouldn't get in a classroom. I knew that Quan would need that reassurance more than ever because he was about to step into a world filled with hurt, pain, and hardship.

It didn't take long for Quan to come home with eyes full of tears and a heavy heart. It didn't take long for him to discover how mean others can be. It didn't take long for him to experience how difficult it can be living with a medical condition that alters your physical appearance.

At school, other school children noticed Quan's enlarged head and picked at him. They called him all kinds of names—grape head, water head, big head, etc., and they laughed at him whenever he came around. Some of the school children treated Quan as if he had a contagious disease. They not only tried to avoid playing with him but they even tried to

Chapter 6: Desperation

avoid being touched by him. I had to be there to answer Quan's questions: "Why are they picking on me? Why do they treat me the way they do? Why don't they like me? What's wrong with me? Do I have to go to school?" I had to wipe away the tears from his eyes while holding back the anger in my heart. I was angry—angry at the cruel kids in that school, angry at the adults who seemed to be just as ridiculous and insensitive as the children, angry at the situation altogether.

Some things we can come to expect, although we never fully get used to them. Being stared at everywhere Quan and I went was one of those things. It didn't matter where we went, people would stop and stare at Quan, both young and old. We felt very uncomfortable out in public, but I was determined to not allow fear to cage us and keep Quan and me living inside a bubble. In the park, people would point and stare, their lips moving while their eyes locked on us. I didn't have to imagine what they were saying; I already knew. Everyone seemed as if they were shocked at the size of Quan's head. I felt the stares on the backs of our heads as we walked in public—people just looking, staring, and acting as if they'd seen an alien or something.

In the mall, I can recall an incident where a couple of teenagers were walking by, and when they spotted Quan, one of them hollered out loud, "Damn, he got a big head!" They began to laugh and poke fun at Quan in my face. I stopped them and explained that my son had a condition that caused his head to be enlarged. I also remember a lady in a store staring at Quan's head so much while pushing her shopping cart that she ran into another person. I had another lady ask me once if Quan was in a gang because of all the markings on his head, not realizing those marks were from all the incisions made by surgeons. On another occasion, I took Quan to Chucky Cheese and happened to be sitting next to a group of women who I heard talking about my son. Of course, they didn't know that I was his mother. I overheard one of the ladies saying, "I can tell that there's something wrong with his head. There's something wrong with him." I realized that it was all just a case of misunderstanding, that it was the natural curiosity of people rising to the surface. I realized that people didn't mean to be cruel, and in some cases, they didn't even realize they were being offensive. All of those experiences became eye-openers for me.

They taught me that compassion is something we must learn, that understanding is something we have to strive for, and that sometimes it's worth educating people but other times, there is no need to waste your breath—just keep on moving. Perhaps, the number one thing those experiences taught me was to be patient with others, realizing that the real sickness we must deal with in life is not some physical ailment but the disease of ignorance, that being much more difficult to treat. During this time, however, my resolve grew stronger. I understood that it wasn't Quan who ultimately suffered from a problem but rather those who wallowed in ignorance. Quan began to catch on to the vision as well, thanks to our little talks and prayers. We began to understand that life is filled with problems and that a sickness doesn't mean you're sick; it just means you have a particular challenge to face, a particular burden to bear, a particular story to tell, a certain victory to secure. It just means you have a unique challenge that defines you as an individual and determines your worth.

Chapter 6: Desperation

After seeing the situation in that way, there were no more questions of why, no more nights spent pitying myself because of my situation, and no more fears with regards to others' opinions. After seeing things in a new light, I was ready to face the world with an energy and a zest I had never experienced before. Quan's birth gave me a newfound sense of purpose, but his struggle developed character in me like never before. I could see me changing. I could feel it. I could see rays of light beginning to pierce through the dark of confusion in my soul. That internal change was what I needed the most.

Chapter 6
DESPERATION

As if dealing with Quan's situation wasn't bad enough, there was still life to deal with. Life tugged on my shirttail to remind me that it was still present and that I couldn't devote all my time to helping Quan overcome his personal struggles. Nothing reminded me more that I had other obligations to see about than the eviction notice I received. I truly wished I could have gathered up the money from somewhere somehow to remain in my apartment, but I couldn't, so I got kicked out. I'd fallen behind in my rent. Much of my money had gone to medical expenses. No need to argue and complain. Hey, everyone must eat... including the workers at the rent office.

Quan was a little fighter. He would not quit fighting for his right to live and be happy. Despite being picked on at school, he had a strong enough foundational understanding of his identity—knowing that God loved him and created him and that he was loved and cherished by certain others— to weather the storm in his life. He extended the olive branch of friendship and still made friends. He fought to be accepted as an individual and found peers who accepted him as such. In the meantime, there was a battle on another front I had to face and defeat: the ability to make a living.

    I wanted to do other things with my life. I wanted to be something in life. I decided that it was time for me to go to school and set out on a career path. I was contemplating two options: being a nurse or being a mortician. I decided to pursue nursing. I enrolled in community college and received my certificate in Patient Care Assistance (PCA) and then enrolled in nursing school. While doing this, I was able to get a job at a health care living facility, but I found it difficult to attend classes and maintain the right GPA because I still had to focus on Quan. Just when I was getting into the swing of things, Quan suddenly needed surgery, or there was some other situation concerning Quan's condition that would arise that would pull my mind away from school. So more often than not, I found myself having to be excused from class to see about Quan.

    This went on and on until finally, I just had to withdraw from classes altogether. My professors were understanding and even sympathetic towards me, but they had to continue with class; they couldn't hold up the others just for me. I even attempted to enroll in online classes, but I still found it difficult to complete the assignments because I was exhausted from dealing with Quan's situation. I had to drop out of that school. By now, I had burned the financial aid bridge so to

Chapter 7: The Dream

speak, and I knew I wouldn't be allowed to keep applying for financial aid. There was no need to get upset with anyone or anything; it was just life.

Once again, I ended up putting school on hold while attending to other matters. Not only that, but I lost my job because the position I was in was no longer needed at that facility. So now, I was out of school and unemployed, but I still had to tend to my son and mother, both of whom were dealing with serious illnesses. I had to figure out ways to keep *myself* out of the hospital now! The stress of daily living was enough, without adding Quan's and mom's conditions to the equation.

PLAYING HOUSE

There were some things I put on hold, but my relationship with Mike wasn't one of those things. We were still hot and heavy, and perhaps, due to all the stress I was under, we'd become even hotter and heavier. Sweat poured off me like water in the clubs as I danced away the day, and at night, sweat poured even more in the bedroom as Mike stroked my worries away time and time again. Mike knew how to make me feel good, how to take my mind off everything. I truly desired those moments where I could feel like a woman again rather than a caretaker. I wanted to let my hair down and feel the sympathetic breezes blowing through the strands of my hair. I longed to feel my wild side, to be untamed and loose. It didn't matter to me at the time that Mike and I weren't married. All that mattered to me was that Mike was there for me sexually, financially, and emotionally.

Without realizing it, I had slipped into one of those traps that women dread, telling myself those lies women fear telling themselves, and wearing that label every woman fears wearing after a while. I simply became a baby momma, a friend. I'd even hate to utter the other label I feared drawing near: booty call. I was in a relationship where there was no real commitment.

Days turned into weeks, weeks into months, months into years. Yes, years had gone by, and Mike and I were simply acting like a married couple, though we weren't one. Mike and I, during this time, went on to conceive three more children. I ended up having a miscarriage with the first baby when I was seven weeks pregnant. I had conceived that one when Quan was three years old. Although disappointed, I wasn't devastated; I was actually somewhat relieved. I wasn't prepared for another baby at that time. I could barely take care of the child I already had. I could barely take care of myself.

I was already on the verge of losing my job because I could hardly work consistently; I had to attend to Quan. The boss was riding my back and getting on me about my many absences from work. Again, I understood—the company couldn't hold up its productivity and jeopardize its standing just because of me and my personal issues. Eventually, my job ended up letting me go. I then found myself unemployed and having to deal with an eviction… and my car note was behind several months, so my car was in repossession status. Any moment now, the repo man would be pulling up and confiscating my only vehicle. But Quan still had to go to his appointments at the medical center, my mom still needed her medication, our family still required the necessities. Life had to continue. At least Mike had a car.

Another year had passed, and I was still managing to

CHAPTER 7: THE DREAM

get by the best way I could. It's during times like those that I imagined myself swinging from a pole. *Man, it's just a job... nah!* Trust me, you begin to entertain all kinds of thoughts when you're in a tight spot. I certainly did. Mike and I were still doing our thing, pretending to be married. Another year now, and he still hadn't mentioned marriage. *How much longer will this go on? Better yet, how much longer will I allow it to continue? How much longer will I put up with it? How much longer will I accept excuses and compromise the one thing I do have – my sense of dignity and self-worth.* Not that my sense of importance was based on a man, but it can be disappointing to have a child and live a life of pretend with someone who wants your body but doesn't want to make the same level of sacrifice you have made for them. After a while, the feeling that you get is one where you feel as if you're just using your body to get your bills paid and your hair laid; it's the feeling of prostituting yourself. I still wanted to be treated with respect and valued as a woman, and that meant seeing me as more than a good sexual partner, more than a sex object.

I was thinking tough , but when Mike came around, we continued with business as usual. I didn't want to press the issue of marriage and commitment too much and then end up scaring him off. I just couldn't pull myself to that place of demanding respect... even after Mike and I conceived yet another child. This was baby number three, and certain images of myself began to emerge in my mind after conceiving this child. I wish I could say they were positive images, but they weren't. I saw an image of my mother in my mind – a house full of babies and no man in the house, the portrait of that single mother standing in a cluttered, crowded house, brawly and strong because she must be, wallowing in hard living with no dreams. The fire in her eyes diminished because of too many dreams deferred. The shell of her body fueled by nothing but a compulsion to survive. That was the image I began to see—it was a glimpse of who I was allowing myself to become. I didn't want to be that woman.

I appreciate women who do what it takes to survive, but I didn't want to be one who merely survived; I wanted to be one who thrived. I wanted to dream and follow my dreams. That's one thing I never lost: an understanding that God designed for each of us to have life and life "more abundantly." That means it's not enough to simply exist; you must exist to serve your purpose in life, to live a life that impacts others in such a way that it improves the quality of life for everyone you meet. I learned this in church, and perhaps that's why I couldn't be comfortable with simply settling. I believed I was entitled to more. I believe I am entitled to more. I will always believe I'm entitled to more. This is the hope and the faith instilled in me as a child, and it was and is the hope and faith that drive me even today.

I, unfortunately, experienced another miscarriage, and just like before, I had mixed emotions. On the one hand, I felt a sense of relief over the fact that I didn't have to deal with the responsibility of raising another child while barely being able to take care of myself and Quan, but on the other hand, I felt somewhat sad that a life was lost. As usual, thoughts began to surge through my mind. *Is there something wrong with me? Am I cursed? Is God whipping me, or is He protecting me?* Those were questions worth asking, especially that last one. Definitely, that last one.

Chapter 7
THE DREAM

HER LITTLE BROWN EYES WERE LOOKING DIRECTLY at me, piercing through my soul. You could feel the silence around us, clothing us like a garment. It was a moment of mystique. This little girl standing before me didn't say anything; she just stared at me and allowed her eyes to speak what her heart was bursting at the seams to say. I observed her curly black hair, her smooth brown skin, her little petite frame. The thought, *I know you*, leaped from a place deep within my subconscious mind—from my spirit. *I know you*. She seemed to have heard my thought as I noticed that those eyes were mine, that little face was mine, those little lips were mine. Her eyes communicated the sweetest sense of love. Then suddenly, without warning, a shadowy somberness crept into the area where we were. The darkness seemed to obscure her little face. It was as if she was being erased before my very eyes, fading into limbo. At that moment, panic gripped my heart. I screamed for that little girl to come back, my heart longing to see her again. Just then, I woke up. I sprang up out of bed, my heart thudding inside my chest. I had seen this little girl several times in my dreams, although I never talked about her to anyone. She, much like this chapter in my life, remained hidden, a secret tucked away in the crevices of my existence, no one knowing about it but God.

SO WHAT!

It was rare that I'd try to dodge a call from my godmother, Mrs. Jones. Again, she was my angel, a Godsend. Because of her, I had been able to make it through so much. But at this point in my life, there were some lectures I knew I had coming to me that I didn't want to hear… although I knew I needed to hear them. I didn't want to hear the truth.

I didn't want to be confronted with the ugliness of the bed I had made for myself during this time in my life. I didn't want to hear any talk about my living arrangement. So what, I was "shacking" (as the old folks would call it)! So what, we were just laying up in bed having sex with no plan for the future and with no real prospect of having a future together! So what, we were simply living for the moment! That was my attitude. As long as Mike helped to keep the lights on, I was fine, I thought. By then, ultimatums and deadlines had been tossed out the window. If this was to be, then so be it; I'd just lay up in bed and have babies. *Eventually, I'll get on my feet. Eventually, I'll jump out of this type of living. Eventually.*

When would "eventually" come? I didn't know. But the scary thing was that the more time progressed, the less I

Chapter 8: Coming Out Of Darkness

started to care. I was surviving; that's all that mattered. At that point, I was actually fine being disconnected from the positive people in my life like Mrs. Jones because I felt there was no way they could really understand what I was going through anyway.

It had been a while since I had stepped foot in the church. I decided to trade God for an arrangement. Who needs faith? I got Mike! This was more of a subconscious mentality I began to harbor. Without realizing it, I was telling myself I was in total control and had the power to snap out of my current mentality, but the truth was that I was surrendering power over my life to fear and desperation and allowing myself to settle for less. I had to fool myself into thinking otherwise, and that's why I insulated my ears, that's why I didn't want to go to church, the place where I had received so many affirmations and so much confirmation about God's love and purpose and involvement in my life. Church was the place where I had received so many words of prophecy that hoisted my spirit out of a state of depression and worry. I had become comfortable with less and didn't want to move because I wasn't trusting God anymore. It was as if I had forgotten how many times God provided for me when I prayed. I had begun to ponder the idea that I had let God down, and that only added yet another layer of shame and fear to the equation, one that didn't serve me well.

My spiritual life had been reduced to a mere routine that lacked the passion that once fueled it. I traded that passion for the comfort of convenience. God was an honorable mention in my life, not the love of my life like He had been before. I knew better; I just didn't sense any immediate danger. Perhaps, I was overcome by the fallacy that time was on my side, that I had my whole life ahead of me. I had grown up with the belief that any day could be my last and that I didn't need to play dice with my soul, that death was always lurking around the corner waiting to snag the souls of men at any time, and if not prepared to stand before God upon our deaths, there was a burning hell waiting for us. But now I had become much more relaxed about that. Fear didn't drive me out of the arms of my sinfulness. Unfortunately, I embraced my lifestyle while vaguely recalling from time to time that adage, "God sees everything that we do." But so what if He did! *I'm not planning on dying anytime soon*, I thought to myself. How foolish was I?

You'd think that by now I would have gotten the message that life is not totally in my control, that the future is not in my grasp – unexpected pregnancies and unexpected miscarriages, a string of unforeseen circumstances such as my family members' sicknesses and the associated responsibilities that I hadn't asked for, unplanned hardships like two repossessions and two evictions. By now, you'd think I'd know that there was only one thing certain in life: God hears and answers prayer. And yet, there I was, acting as if I could grab fate by the collar and make it yield to my will, acting as if death was on my schedule. I was living in sin, as the old folks say, and according to the teachings of the Bible, had death crept in and seized hold of me, the only place I would have spent my eternity was a pit in hell. Sadly, I was enjoying the ride there.

THE SECRET

n t I was looking for somewhere to live because I had no place

Chapter 8: Coming Out Of Darkness

of my own to stay. I didn't even have my own transportation. I had to depend totally on Mike to get around and make it during this time in my life, or at least that's what I told myself. I can understand why some women stay in situations that are mentally, emotionally, spiritually, and even physically unhealthy for them. I can understand why some women hold their tongues and grunt under their breaths while fuming at the thought of having to perform and pretend to enjoy something they hate. I can understand. It's about survival, but that survival is fueled by fear, not faith. Trusting God and doing the right thing is always easier said than done. It is a lot easier to take the wrong path, the one that yields instant gratification but long-term damaging effects.

Hot, steamy nights always demanded something of me. I can't say that they demanded as much out of Mike. Concerning myself, I had to deal with the burden of depression and the burden of guilt. It was my body that experienced the sickness, the bleeding, the trauma. It was my mind that harbored the deepest and most condemning thoughts. Now things were about to get a whole lot worse, for on this particularly hot and steamy night, Mike and I would conceive a child once again. Again, this was the worst time for us to be reckless, but we weren't thinking about the consequences of our actions nor their ramifications. I would once again end up on the suffering end.

When unable to see our way through or out of a tough situation, it amazes me (when I think about it even now) how readily assessable trouble is. And many times, trouble will appear to be a heavenly solution. I began to ponder an old possibility, an old solution that I was given to an inconvenient situation. What I said I'd never do, I did.

There wasn't a whole lot to do in Augusta, Georgia. There was some development, but for the most part, it was just a small country town, a tight-knit community. Like Sandersville, there was a lot of farmland and undeveloped land covered with trees. It was just a small, quiet town. But even in Augusta, Georgia, you could find a Planned Parenthood clinic. I drove down to that clinic, fighting through all the hesitation and reservations I had along the way. Every fiber of my being screamed at me, telling me to turn around and not venture through the doors of that clinic. But I found myself breaking a rule I swore I'd never break just for the sake of comfort and convenience. The less I turned to God for His guidance, the less I put my trust in Him to take care of me, the more I was doing things I thought I'd never do and contemplating things I never thought I'd contemplate. I felt myself venturing further and further down a strange, dark path.

After the abortion, I left the clinic, my mind swirling with mixed emotions. Unlike the time after the two miscarriages I experienced prior to this, my heart and mind were vexed with a guilt I'd never experienced before. This time the termination of life was voluntary. I chose to end the pregnancy. It was my decision to end a life. I just couldn't deal with all of the pressure that came with raising a new baby multiplied with the problem of homelessness, sick loved ones, and financial hardship... not to mention a shaky relationship with a man who didn't seem to want to commit to stable a relationship (in other words, get married).

I hid the news of the abortion from everyone. The only other person who knew about it was Mike. We had both

Chapter 8: Coming Out Of Darkness

agreed on the abortion, but I privately carried the guilt of it in my soul. My faith as a Christian teaches that abortion is a sin, that it is the act of murder. This, I wrestled with night after night. I wore the label in my mind, in my heart. At first, there were the arguments fed to me by the Planned Parenthood workers playing in my head, telling me that I was not committing murder, that I was not really killing a human being, that I was actually making the best decision for myself. I must admit that every one of those arguments sounded good, so reassuring and comforting, their proponents so convincing.

There were two problems though. First off, the Planned Parenthood clinicians didn't prepare me for the physical damage the abortion would have on my body. I ended up experiencing a condition called endometriosis, a painful disorder where the tissue that normally lines the inside of the uterus—the endometrium—grows outside of the uterus. This condition is accompanied by intense pelvic pains and irregular menstrual cycles. The second problem was none of those Planned Parenthood workers could be there with me during the late nights I lay awake in bed dealing with the heaviness in my heart. Their arguments couldn't soothe that part of me (my soul) which carried an internal knowing, a natural intuition, a special discernment within. That part of me was saying otherwise. It was dismissing the arguments suggested to me by all the Planned Parenthood staff. In my spirit, I knew what I did was wrong. Call it a hunch. Call it the conviction of the Holy Spirit. Whatever you want to call it, it was loudly ringing in my soul, leaving a conviction that could only be wiped away through honest confession and heartfelt repentance.

THE SECRET IS OUT

It was Thanksgiving Day, and my godmother, Mrs. Jones, was coming to visit and spend some time with my family and me. I was glad to see her, but I was also really nervous about seeing her. I was even uneasy about looking her directly in the eyes, knowing that I had done something she would greatly disapprove of. I didn't want to break her heart with the news of my abortion. I already knew what she'd say and think about it.

When Mrs. Jones arrived, I greeted her with gladness. We hugged and we talked. We talked about all kinds of things. As was typical, Mrs. Jones was checking up on me to make sure I was taking care of my responsibilities as a young woman: seeing about my son, taking good care of myself, staying out of trouble, budgeting and saving money, being responsible, etc. I, of course, responded with the typical affirmative yet vague answers, so as not to alert her that I was not doing so well nor being so responsible. But then Mrs. Jones hit me with a curveball. "Girl, you done picked up some weight. Are you pregnant?" Mrs. Jones asked. My heart rate escalated at that moment. Nervousness gripped me. I almost froze in my tracks, looking like a deer in the headlights. I couldn't lie to my godmother; I didn't know how to, at least, not convincingly.

"Oh, I'm on birth control—that Depo-Provera shot," I responded. Mrs. Jones just looked at me, almost as if sensing that there was something I wasn't telling her, something more that I needed to add. I felt the compulsion to confess to Mrs. Jones what I had done, but I kept fighting back the urge.

Chapter 8: Coming Out Of Darkness

Finally, unable to hold my peace, I came out and explained to her: "No, I'm not pregnant. Actually... I got an abortion a few months ago." After telling her that, Mrs. Jones just broke down in tears, sobbing. The pain from her heart was resonating strongly with me. She was crushed by the news. I was, on the other hand, somewhat relieved that I finally got the secret off my chest. The pressure of holding onto it was killing me. I could pretend as if everything was alright at home and at other places, but like the Bible says in Ephesians chapter 5: Everything done in the darkness will eventually come to the light. Eventually. Better sooner than later.

DEALING WITH THE GUILT AND THE SHAME

Shortly after my abortion, I started having dreams about that curly-haired little girl I introduced to you earlier. I knew who she was. I knew. This was something supernatural, something that let me know there are deeper mechanics and dynamics operating behind the scenes in our lives than what is realized by modern science. The little girl I aborted visited me in my dreams. She wasn't a little girl I miscarried. She was the one I chose to abort. I could see the sadness in her heart; it was a feeling of being robbed of a chance at life. This began to eat me up inside; it brought tears streaming down my face night after night. The conviction I felt behind my abortion kept building as the days progressed until I couldn't resist crying out to God for forgiveness. I cried out to God one night in the solitude of isolation and He spoke into my spirit these simple words: "You are forgiven. All things work together for the good of them that love Me." As simple as that, a heavy weight lifted off me. I sensed that the weight I was carrying was spiritual. Sure, it might have been suppressed with psychiatric drugs and treatments, but it couldn't be lifted any other way than through the spiritual act of repentance.

It was during that time that the reality of the spirit world became more real to me. I realized that sin carries a heavy price, one that often affects our psychological, emotional, and even our physical well-being. Many people aren't really in need of medication; they're in need of prayer and repentance. They can't seem to put their finger on the true source of the affliction and anguish they're experiencing, and that is because no one has informed them that there's an aspect of the human experience that science has yet to discover: the spiritual. This is, perhaps, the biggest and most real aspect of our being.

In the upcoming days, I had to continue to fight away the feelings of guilt and shame in me as a result of the abortion… and the other sins I had committed. God was still speaking to me, even in the midst of it. One Bible verse the Holy Spirit kept bringing up in my spirit was Romans 8:1, which says, "There is therefore now no condemnation for those who are in Christ Jesus" (ESV). This Bible verse helped me so much; it brought an unspeakable sense of relief into my soul. I would quote this verse to myself every day. I had to because there was another power, I sensed, that was hoping to drown me in the spirit of depression over my mistakes. The reality that my mistakes didn't define me but that God would rather use them to further mature me in life was the reassurance I needed the most. I may make mistakes, but I'm not a mistake. I may fall, but I'm not a failure. God knows how to wrap His humongous arms around our feeble spirits and squeeze us like

Chapter 8: Coming Out Of Darkness

a dad, not casting us away because of our shortcomings but helping us to rise above them and learn from them. That's the love of the Father. That's what made me fall in love with God all over again. It wasn't the fear of hell and eternal torment (although those are real) that drove me closer to God; it was His unfailing love.

MIRACLE SICKNESS

Even our problems serve to bless us when we put them in God's hands. That was a valuable lesson I learned from an unexpected experience. It was somewhat interesting—I would even dare say miraculous—how I ended up being right by Mrs. Jones' side during her final days on this earth.

Back in 2010, Mrs. Jones ended up being hospitalized because of complications with her heart. She had to have a heart catheterization. Upon discovering that she was sick, I immediately jumped in my car and drove all the way to Raleigh-Durham, North Carolina, to visit her in the hospital. When I got to her room, it broke my heart to see her just lying in that hospital bed looking so helpless, so sick. A wave of unwanted feelings tried to come over me, feelings I refused to entertain. There I was looking at a scene that was somewhat familiar, facing a situation I refused to accept as a possibility.

When I entered Mrs. Jones' room, she was glad to see me, too. She greeted me with a big smile. I gave her a hug and expressed how important it was for me to see her, that nothing could have prevented me from being there by her side—and I do mean nothing. And in her motherly fashion, Mrs. Jones looked at me lovingly and shared these words of encouragement: "You know, you turned out to be a very nice young lady. You're a good mother to your son. And I thank God for you being in my life," she said to me. She continued to pour out her heart to me... as if leaving me with parting words. To me, it would have been preferable that she saved those words and simply bounced back from that sickness in the fullness of strength. I would have wanted to see her waltz out of that hospital like she was on top of the world, with no "goodbyes" because that time wasn't upon us. My prayers were militant. I just knew that God would not allow Mrs. Jones to go anywhere... especially since I demanded that she be healed. I mean, God answered just about every other prayer I prayed, so why not this one?

There are those times when your faith isn't tested, but rather, it's clarified in your life. During those times, you discover that God is the one with the ultimate plan and foresight, not us. This was one of those times. I would discover that God truly does move in mysterious ways. Rather than Mrs. Jones getting healed during my visitation with her, I got sick.

I suddenly and mysteriously developed a kidney stone. While at the hospital, I started feeling sharp, unbearable pains in my abdomen, side, and groin area. I complained to the doctor about what I was feeling, at which point they gave me a few examinations. After the test results came in, they admitted me into the hospital. Suddenly, I went from being a visitor to being a patient. A sudden problem produced an opportunity for me to stay by Mrs. Jones' side during the rest of the time she was in that hospital. I enjoyed leaving out of my room to go upstairs to see her. I was on the first floor and she was on the fourth. One day, we just sat and talked for a good while. We talked about a lot, and it's amazing when I think about it

Chapter 8: Coming Out Of Darkness

today. My plan was to get back on the road and head back to Georgia after paying a visit to Mrs. Jones, and my expectation was for her to bounce back after this experience and be around for a little while longer, at least a few more years. But my sudden sickness forced me to stay at that hospital with Mrs. Jones, not realizing that would be my last time opportunity to spend time with her.

One night I pressed my way up to Mrs. Jones' room, despite feeling pains coursing through my body. I moved slowly, in a staggering fashion. When she saw me, she said, "I thank you for all that you've done for me. I love you! I love you! I love you!" Tears began to stream down my cheeks as she talked. Perhaps, she was sensing that her time was drawing near and that she didn't have a lot of time to say what she needed to say. Whatever the case, a week later the lights went out in her eyes as she took her final breath and gave up her spirit to God. In May of 2010, Mrs. Jones, my angel, passed away. She went to her home on high.

There is, perhaps, no one else (besides my own mother and grandmother) who has had such a profound effect and impact on my life. Mrs. Jones was truly a necessary part of my life, especially during the years when I needed the wisdom to deal with my son. It was during those times that I needed the strength, the aid, the assistance of every angel, both visible and invisible, that God could send… and some more.

Woman Of Persistent Faith

Chapter 8
COMING OUT OF DARKNESS

SOMETIMES BEFORE THE THINGS AROUND US CAN CHANGE, we must change. My situation hadn't changed much. I was still in dire straits financially, practically homeless, car-less, unemployed, trying to take care of a special needs child and see about a sick mother, and hoping to receive a marriage proposal... but it was my rekindled interest in God, my rededication to Him, my revived willingness to do things His way that ignited a new fire in me. My mind was returning. My strength as an individual was returning. My dignity as a woman was being restored. My confidence, hope, optimism and resolve were being reestablished. I was starting to feel a sense of joy, peace, and self-respect again. I knew I was back on track.

Emerging from a pit of deep depression and shame, I was now determined to fight for my promised future. I knew God had a plan for my life and for Quan's life; I just needed to put an end to my self-loathing and self-pitying and fight for it. I realized that Quan's survival was tied to my faith; therefore, I began to get up every morning and speak positive affirmations over myself. I began to quote the Word of God over my life and Quan's life daily, choosing to believe that the best was yet to come. I chose to take on a positive outlook again. Faith became the weapon I used to dismember the darkness around me and the fear that was trying to cripple me. Faith kept me alive so I could keep Quan alive.

During that time in my life, I became much more conscious of what I listened to. I made sure not to entertain anything that would thrust me back into that place of depression I had just escaped from. I discovered one fundamental principle during this time: In order to build faith, you must surround yourself with the people and things of God. You have to be in the right place. You can't develop faith in God while hanging around people who are filled with doubt, fear, and carnality. If faith, according to Hebrews 11:6, is the only thing that can get God's attention and please Him and produce the miracle that you need, then it is important that you do everything necessary to grow your faith. To be honest, I can't stress this point enough.

I began to attend church regularly again. And of course, there were those moments when there were things said during the preacher's messages that left a stinging feeling in my heart. I would feel convicted when the minister talked about sin, especially sexual sin (fornication) or when he dwelled on the topic of murder, citing Exodus 20:13 which says, "Thou shalt not murder," but it didn't condemn me anymore because the Holy Spirit had reminded me that my past sins were forgiven and that I now had a clean slate. I didn't have to worry about the things I had done because all of that was behind me now. I knew that, according to the Bible, one of the signs of God's love is that He will correct us, chastise us if He must, do whatever it takes to keep us out of the grip of demonic activity and oppression. If that means He must convict us, He will. If that means He must allow us to learn things the hard way, He will. One Bible verse I remembered is Hebrews 12:6, which says, "...the Lord disciplines the ones he loves..." In order to get better, in order to become a better person, in order to grow in faith and mature as an individual, I needed discipline, I needed correction. Those are the only things that can truly change us from within.

    A major source of encouragement at that time was my pastor and his wife, Bishop Mark and Dorothy Walden. They would pray with me and constantly remind me that my situation was in God's hands. They would remind me that God was going to use my situation, my story, and Quan's disability to encourage others who may experience the same or similar situations. With faith rising in my spirit, worry began to disappear. It was as if I had the freedom to relax and let go of all of the wrong beliefs I held: thinking I was responsible for things being the way they were; thinking it was my responsibility to change my situation; even thinking I had the power to change things in my life. I could now trust that God, who has the power, ability, and responsibility to take care of Quan and me, was going to honor His promises in His Word.

GETTING BACK UP

The night was long, but things were beginning to turn around in my life, and they were turning around quickly. God knew I needed a source of income and a place to stay. I prayed to Him for direction and immediately realized that I needed to go and apply for disability for Quan. Without delay, I went and applied to the Social Security Administration (SSA) for Quan's disability. At first, he was denied disability, so I did an appeal. During that appeal process, Quan had to have another surgery—this was his eleventh shunt revision. After having his eleventh surgery for the same thing, the SSA decided to approve our application for disability for Quan.

I was thankful to God for this assistance, as it would provide Quan and me with $400 a month. Although $400 wasn't a whole lot of money, it was a lot more than what I was making, which was zero dollars. Also, Medicaid paid for Quan's surgeries, so I didn't have to deal with that medical bill nightmare which would have eaten me alive. The blessings didn't stop there. Quan's grandmother surprisingly came through for Quan and me with a big blessing. She knew the manager at the Housing Authority and managed, through this connection, to get me an apartment where I only had to pay $86 dollars a month. That allowed me to pay my utility bills and still have money left over to live off. I applied for food stamps, which made it possible for Quan and me to be able to keep the refrigerator and the pantry stocked. While Quan and I were receiving assistance from the state, Quan's father, Mike, was also working and contributing to our well-being.

CHAPTER 9: CONVERSATIONS WITH GOD

Rays of sunshine were now piercing through the darkness. Daylight was beginning to break in my life. I really started to get the sense that Quan and I were going to make it.

QUAN'S IMPROVEMENT

As the days went by, Quan began to improve in so many areas. He got much better in his therapy sessions as he began to gain more and more strength. Quan tested out of the Special Ed program and no longer needed an IEP. He was a living miracle. He still had to have speech therapy and receive regular checkups to make sure that the fluid wasn't building up on his brain, but I was amazed to see the improvement he was making. It all inspired me.

HEALED BY HURT AND PAIN

While trying to get on my feet, I found myself amid another whirlwind of chaos: Mike and I were starting to go to war. Our little relationship, which had been holding on by just a string to begin with, was now turning hostile.

I don't know if it was due to jealousy or what, but a lot of crazy chatter started to emerge from the people that were around Mike. Some of his friends—those he trusted—started telling him lies about me. This was hurtful. It stung me deeply because I hadn't done anything to any of these individuals, but for some reason, they felt compelled to involve themselves in the middle of Mike's and my relationship. They started telling Mike that I was cheating on him with other men. Of course, none of this was true, but Mike began to believe what they were telling him, and his attitude began to turn very negative towards me. The seed of resentment was sown by those he called his friends, and .there was nothing I could say to convince him otherwise.

As the days progressed, I would attempt to prove my faithfulness to Mike in whatever way possible. I wanted him to know that I loved him and desired only to be with him, but that seed of resentment germinated and took root deep inside him. He began to be more and more distant. He would look at me with a look of anger at times; other times, he'd have a look of disgust. He would come around to see the baby and would try to pretend that I wasn't standing there. I'd get the silent treatment. When we did talk during that time, it would usually lead to an argument. Mike was playing his little games, trying to get back at me for something he couldn't even prove I did. At first, I would get upset about the way he was treating me. I felt it was unfair, that I deserved a chance to be heard, but after putting up with it for so long, I stopped hoping for the relationship to bounce back and started looking for the exit myself. Now, the tables had turned. By that time, I was a woman who was fed-up, tired of being disrespected, tired of being mistreated, tired of being second place to other people in Mike's life, tired of having to try to prove myself. I was done! My fire was burning out and my passion quickly fading away. I went from being in love to being exhausted with a relationship that was beginning to be more of a burden than a blessing in my life. Mike would always be the father of my son, but I was slowly beginning to accept as a reality the one thing I dreaded: Mike and I were not going to make it as a couple.

In the earlier days, I'd have Kleenexes balled up on my bed filled with my snot and tears while thinking about the days

Chapter 9: Conversations With God

when we were—or at least I was—crazy in love. I'd rest in memories of the two of us, those moments we created together, sitting in the forefront of my mind like a dress in a display window at the mall. To me, my relationship with Mike was an investment of my heart and soul. The bone-crushing reality was what I struggled to accept. The relationship I had worked so hard to build was getting ready to fall apart in my hands. I knew that this chapter in my life was coming to an end but how to let go was an issue. One thing that became apparent, however, is that I *needed* to let go of this relationship. Any relationship can be repaired if both parties involved want to repair it, but if only one person is fighting for the relationship, chances are it won't make it. At some point, it dawned on me that I was the only one fighting for the relationship. I was the only one still hoping and believing and fighting for a future together. Mike, to be honest, had already checked out of the fight. He desired to push me away more than he desired to fight through thoughts and feelings of resentment. He wasn't working with me to recapture the passion that once lived in our hearts for one another.

The fear of being alone was one I was going to have to stomach, face, and conquer. Even greater was the fear of reliving what I had seen my mother go through while I was growing up – letting man after man pass through the doors of her house, each one as baseless and shifty as the wind, gone after the brief moment of sensuality had sizzled out. And then, at the end of the day, she was still alone, holding the fragments of her shattered soul in her hands… and taking out her frustrations on the one close by, which was little ole' me. I'd prefer to be loved, cherished, and held by someone who desired to walk with me along this journey, but I knew, I just knew that it was better to walk alone as opposed to allowing myself to be walked on. So, I confronted Mike one day and laid it all out on the line. I told him what I was feeling, what I was thinking, and what I would no longer tolerate and live with. I'd had enough. We both reached an agreement that it was better for us to simply be friends and not lovers. Both Mike and I knew that we were the best thing for Quan but the worst thing for each other.

After Mike and I broke off the relationship, a weight lifted off my shoulders. No longer did I hold myself hostage to a hope that would never pan out, one that, perhaps, wasn't a part of God's plan for my life to begin with. I don't know... However, I do know that as a result of finally stepping out of the relationship, I was able to breathe a little easier and think a little clearer. At that point, I realized that what I had used as a crutch for so long was actually my handicap. Mike was, and is, a great person. He is a good father. He loves his son. We both take care of our son. We had something special, we did. But I placed too many of my hopes and dreams in him and ended up forgetting about the One who had always been there for me, the One who holds the power to turn my dreams into a reality. That One is my Savior and my Creator, Jesus the Christ.

I thought that I could only be whole with a man. Perhaps that was because of the strained and virtually non-existent relationship that I had with my natural father. An unhealed heart hides behind many justifications. I had never really thought about it before: Why had I desperately clung on to a relationship that was doomed from the beginning? And I wouldn't have ever thought about my situation in a new light had things continued the way they were. Sometimes a bad situation is God's way of revealing a deeper problem, one that must be addressed and dealt with for us to truly be free and move forward into the glorious light of the future God promised us.

Sometimes God will reveal to us through pain and disappointment what's broken on the inside of us. And if we can simply resist the urge to curse the hurt and pain, resist the urge to harbor bitterness and unforgiveness towards the people and situations (the tools that God is using), then we will be able to hear destiny whispering in our spirits in a soft and gentle tone, "This is for your good. God designed this for your good. In the end, you'll be glad this happened, so rejoice."

Only faith—a genuine belief in God and relationship with Him through His Word—can produce such a happiness within amid suffering, loss, and pain. Only God can produce a light in your spirit that can engulf the darkness all around you. Only the Holy Spirit can extract joy out of the hard shell of disappointment and enable us to rejoice in the face of great adversity. Only God.

MORE BUMPS IN THE ROAD

Like a baby trying to walk, the road to recovery is filled with ups and downs, rising and falling, victories and defeats. There will be days when we are doing good while moving forward in life, and then there will be those days when things will happen that seem to knock us back down. As long as we keep moving forward, we will gain the strength to not only walk but run and leap into our destinies. I was doing well at that point, but there was still a good distance ahead of me to cover before I could finally get into a secure spot. And even then, due to the unpredictability of life, I would still have to trust God and walk by faith because I did not know what the next day might hold.

While living in my new apartment and collecting that SSA check and food stamps, I was relaxing and feeling much more comfortable. However, God has a way of moving us out of our comfort zone and propelling us toward destiny. While at that apartment complex, I had one of those nosy neighbors who seemed to have too much time on their hands, and now things were about to change. My neighbor contacted the rent office and reported me to them, telling them that my mother was living in the apartment with me and pointing out that she wasn't on the lease. Because of my neighbor's actions, I was evicted once again from my home and had to find somewhere to live with my sick mother and sick child. I ended up finding a two-bedroom apartment on the other side of town which was only $200 a months. That price still allowed me to pay my rent and have money to live off with Quan's disability, although not as much as before.

I needed more than Quan's disability money in order to take care of my family; I needed a job. Because of that need, I would find myself being uprooted once again from my comfortable little situation. I packed up and got ready to move again, this time to Augusta, Georgia. There I found a job as an office manager at a dental office, thanks to a girlfriend of mine from church who had started her own dental practice. She truly blessed me with that position. She was more than my boss; she was my friend. And she did more than give me a job; she gave me a much-needed push to go back to school and finish pursuing my education in the nursing field. I appreciated God for that push. Taking her advice, I went back to school. I enrolled in a community college there in Augusta and began taking the core classes for nursing. I remained in school until 2013, when Quan began having his surgeries again.

During that time, I ended up totaling the car Mrs. Jones had bought for me. But I didn't lie down and give up; instead, I got up and got another car. A used car. A lemon. Sure, this car was cheap, wasn't really any good, and needed extensive repairs, but that clunker got me from point A to point B.

The one thing that kept me going at that time was my faith, my ability to encourage myself in my faith, my ability to speak positive affirmations over my life daily and not allow any negative thoughts to dwell in my mind. Whenever a negative thought would arise, I would immediately beat it down with affirmations of God's love for me and His plan for my life. This preserved me, fueled me, shielded my mind, and kept me together like glue long enough for me to hold on between blessings. All I needed was to not give up—there was always a blessing just around the corner. Always!

Chapter 9
CONVERSATIONS WITH GOD

THERE WERE A LOT OF WORDS SAID DURING THOSE hellish years between 2007 and 2013 when Quan had his last surgery. I heard nasty insults from strangers who demonstrated a disgusting amount of insensitivity and gall. I received insults from people in church who had high hopes for me only to be disappointed when I walked through the doors of the church with a belly bulging because I was several months pregnant. I had to endure these insults. I had to learn how to smile and pretend to be unaffected by the opinions of others. I had to hold back tears and anger because of the bullying my child endured from his peers. Some of them said the most damaging things to my son to his face. Words hurt.

And it is because of the impact of words on our lives that I decided to engage in a battle of words. If no one else would speak life, I'd speak life. If no one else would encourage Quan and me, I'd do it. I'd stand in the mirror and say, "We're going to make it." If no one else appeared to be optimistic about Quan's future, I'd choose to be optimistic. But thank God for the encouraging words He would send to me through my pastor, through my godmother, and through certain other people. I still realized, however, that at the end of the day, it didn't matter what anyone else said to me about my situation; the only thing that mattered was what I said about my situation. This is faith in action. I had to apply it continuously.

THINGS THEY SAID

I can recall receiving the most frightening news during the time when Quan had yet another shunt revision. n On that day, after ythe operation, Quan was left in a coma. The doctor informed me that he didn't think Quan was going to make it. He was preparing me for the worst. Death. The doctor told me that due to the amount of the pressure and fluid on Quan's brain, the chance of him living after that surgery was slim to none. That's what they said. That type of news is enough to make any mother's heart cave in her chest. It is enough to make any parent feel faint. At those moments, the only thing you can and should do is turn to God. My experience was much like that of King Hezekiah's in the book of 2 Kings 20:2. It tells us after the King Hezekiah received the news that he was about to die, "Hezekiah turned his face to the wall and prayed to the LORD..." Sometimes, you must shut out every-

Chapter 2: Angels

one and everything and get in a place where you can be alone with God and cry out to Him, reminding Him of His promises in His Word. I had to have my own conversations with God during those times; either that, or I would have suffocated in fear and worry.

Another thing I was told by medical doctors was that because of Quan's condition, he would forever be mentally challenged. They said he would never be able to excel or keep up in school with the other kids. This the doctors assured me of. Of course, I didn't want to receive this possibility either; and just like in the case where I was informed of the possibility of Quan's untimely death, I had to find my secret place to go and spend time with God in prayer and remind Him of His Word. Well, as it turns out, the doctors were wrong again. Not only did Quan go on to complete his therapy and graduate high school in normal classes with his peers, but he even was accepted into college. Today, Quan is a student in college and is majoring in premed with the aim of obtaining a degree in neuroscience. That's not so bad for a person doctors said would be "retarded" all his life and would never have the mental capacity to accomplish such goals.

Quan continues to be an inspiration to so many people. He wows and dazzles others with his extraordinary testimony. Sometimes people are speechless after hearing about how many times Quan has undergone the knife and how many times he nearly died. For Quan to still be alive is nothing short of a miracle. Quan not only excelled in school, but he even tutors other students in math. He also lifts the spirits of others through music, as he loves to write music and sing.

QUAN'S CONVERSATION WITH GOD

When I sit back and think about all that God brought Quan and me through, it amazes me. Sometimes I am speechless when I look at Quan, noticing how strong he is, how smart and intelligent he is, how encouraging he is. He has become my inspiration. And I know that all of this is because of the prayers of myself and others that have gone up repeatedly before God on Quan's behalf. But I would be remiss if I left out the fact that Quan also prayed and received his own encouragement and strength from God. He realized that he would need to develop his own personal walk and relationship with God. All I could do was be an example to him of how to make it, but he would have to apply the same principles in his own life that he saw me model before him.

One day Quan relayed a very special message to me. It was 2013 and he had just come out of surgery. While lying in his hospital bed, he asked God, "Lord, why do I have to have so many surgeries?" At that moment, he said the Holy Spirit spoke to him and said, "It will all make sense later." A few days later, as Quan recounts, he was experiencing a lot of pain and he asked God in prayer, "Why am I having so much pain?" God answered and said, "I am allowing you to experience what many people are going through and don't know how to deal with."

"Well," Quan continued, "what is that?" The answer he got from God really stuck with him. The Lord replied, "Many people can deal with the outside pain like bumps, bruises, and scratches, but they can't deal with hurt on the inside. And once they experience the pain, they run away from it, but I'm allowing you to experience the pain so you may

CHAPTER 2: ANGELS

help others. Just like the surgeon had to remove the scar tissue from your stomach, I am trying to remove the scar tissue from around people's hearts. I am mending the broken hearts of many people that are in so much pain which they don't know how to handle!"

When Quan relayed this information to me, my heart was so relieved and encouraged. I knew then that he had the strength and assurance that he needed to make it on his own at that point. If there was one thing I desired more than anything in this world, it was that. I wanted Quan to gain the kind of strength and resolve to make it regardless of what may come or go in his life. Now, my heart was at ease as a mother. I receive strength from my son now, whereas, before this, I had to be his strength. Today, my son prays for me and reminds me of my own destiny.

And speaking of my own destiny, I am back in school, working on my goals. Quan's father and I continue to be good friends. God has continued to open doors for me that are mind-blowing, absolutely incredible. The storm clouds have vanished in my life and the sun is shining again. Today, I'm a stronger person. Today, I'm a better person. Today, I realize that the storm was actually a blessing in disguise, a tool used in the hands of a sovereign God to make Quan and me the miracles He wants to use to let you know—YES, YOU!—that miracles do happen. He's using us to remind you that He will work a miracle in your life and situation if you turn to Him and put your trust, hope, and faith in Him. This book is simply here to remind you of one essential truth: "And we know that for those who love God, all things work together for good, for those who are called according to his purpose"

(Romans 8:28, ESV).

This is my story, the story of physical, mental, and emotional healing. God used my son's illness to heal an illness in my own heart. Then He healed us both when the time came. Today, I'm a better person. My son and I have learned to love, embrace, and accept the things about us that we struggled with. I have learned to embrace my dark complexion, something that I had struggled with from my childhood because of my mother's constant criticism of my appearance. Seeing Quan's strength and his struggle with overcoming a complex due to his appearancee, one marred by the many scars on his head from all the incisions, helped me to gain strength. Learning to gain compassion for my son's antagonists actually cultivated in me a compassion for my own. While helping my son get healed from the pain in his heart, I ended up getting healed myself. God was washing away all the negative words, all the lies, all the criticism, all the pain that held me bound, even secretly, during this process. He was teaching Quan and me the true meaning of Psalm 139:14, which says, "I will praise thee; for I am fearfully and wonderfully made; marvelous are thy works; and that my soul knoweth right well."

Persistent faith brought me to the place in life where I am today. It was persistent faith that brought me to this spot where I'm looking at a sordid past behind me and a road bending over the horizon of a bright future before me. Today, I'm smiling and I'm happy, knowing I have the freedom to live and pursue every dream that God placed in my heart, knowing that I can overcome every future obstacle that stands in my way, knowing that God is always seeking to not only provide me with a miracle but also make me a miracle in every

Chapter 2: Angels

situation. And because God made Quan and me a miracle, we are here to remind you that there is a miracle with your name on it. Yes, there is! Speak it today! Believe it! Claim it! God is waiting for you to believe Him for it. He's waiting for you to allow Him to transform your life into a miracle that will bless the lives of others as well.

ABOUT THE AUTHOR

Akiesha "KeKe" Taylor is an active member at her church, The House of GOD COGIC! She has a passion to serve others and be a vessel for GOD.

KeKe is currently furthering her education by pursuing a degree in Theology at Seminary! In her spare time she loves to encourage parents who are raising kids with disabilities, listening to music, journaling, and spending time with her son, Quan.

To contact Akiesha "KeKe" Taylor,
send your email to:
akieshat@gmail.com

www.ingramcontent.com/pod-product-compliance
Lightning Source LLC
Chambersburg PA
CBHW021134300426
44113CB00006B/418